# Creepy crawlies

# INTRODUCTION

One group of creepy crawlies, the insects, are the most successful animals on Earth. So far, scientists have managed to identify around 1.5 million different types of insects. There is no part of the globe, nor any habitat, where insects cannot live, and there are even a few kinds of insects that live in the sea. Some scientists think that there might actually be another 30 million kinds of insects yet to be identified!

Not all creepy crawlies are insects however; there are spiders, woodlice, centipedes, and millipedes among others. People often mistake these creatures for insects, but all insects have six legs while spiders have eight; wood lice have ten; and centipedes many more. And then there are slugs, snails, worms and other creatures which slither.

Look around you; you'll find creepy crawlies in all sorts of places you might not expect!

## How to use your i-SPY book

The creepy crawlies in this book are arranged in groups, from slugs and snails through to flies and pond creatures. We've usually shown the adult insect in the book, but if you know what their young look like and you spy one, you can score for that instead. Where identification of a species is very difficult, the scientific name of the wider species family or order has been used. The abbreviation spp. means plural of species. You need 1000 points to send off for your i-SPY certificate (see page 64) but that is not too difficult because there are masses of points in every book. Each entry has a star or circle and points value beside it. The stars represent harder to spot entries. As you make each i-SPY, write your score in the circle or star. For entries where there is a question, double your score if you can answer it. Answers are shown on page 63.

**Points: 5**
double with answer

## BRANDLING WORM

**Scientific name**
*Eisenia foetida*

Not all earthworms live in the soil. Brandling Worms live in compost and other decaying matter. They produce a pungent liquid when disturbed.

*What do earthworms feed on?*

## GARDEN SNAIL

**Points: 5**

**Scientific name**
*Cornu aspersum*

You are most likely to find snails on the move after it has rained, or if you go out into the garden as it is getting dark. They prefer to stay hidden if the weather is hot.

## BANDED SNAIL

**Points: 15**

**Scientific name**
*Cepaea nemoralis*

There are a number of different species of Banded Snail, yellow, brown or pink, with or without bands. Look for them in gardens, hedgerows or on sand dunes.

 **Points: 15**

## GREAT GREY SLUG

**Scientific name**
*Limax maximus*

Like snails, slugs tend to come out after rain or in the cool of the evening. They are sometimes known as leopard slugs due to their spots.

## GREAT BLACK SLUG

**Points: 10**

**Scientific name**
*Arion ater*

This slug can be black, brown or orange. Slugs feed on the stems, roots and leaves of plants, making them very unpopular with farmers and gardeners.

Points: 10

## AZURE DAMSELFLY

Scientific name
*Coenagrion puella*

These damselflies are common around ponds and lakesides during the summer. While the males always display the azure blue colour, the females are usually green.

## LARGE RED DAMSELFLY

Points: 10
double for the wheel position

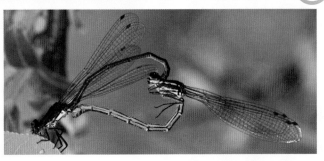

Scientific name
*Pyrrhosoma nymphula*

The earliest of the damselflies appear from late spring onwards. This pair is mating in what is called the 'wheel position'.

## BEAUTIFUL DEMOISELLE DAMSELFLY

**Points: 15**

**Scientific name** *Calopteryx virgo*

Look out for the Demoiselle Damselflies. They live beside ponds, lakes, canals, rivers and streams, but they hunt away from water and may end up in your back garden.

**Points: 10**

## COMMON DARTER DRAGONFLY

**Scientific name** *Sympetrum striolatum*

While damselflies hold their wings over the body at rest, dragonflies hold them out to the side. The Common Darter male is red but the female is more of a yellow colour.

## BROAD-BODIED CHASER DRAGONFLY

**Points: 15**

**Scientific name**
*Libellula depressa*

This lovely dragonfly is in the habit of visiting and even breeding in garden ponds. While the male is blue the female is golden in colour.

**Points: 25**　　　Top Spot!

## GOLDEN-RINGED DRAGONFLY

**Scientific name**
*Cordulegaster boltonii*

This is one of the large darter dragonflies, with a wingspan that can measure up to 10 cm across. They usually live near moving water where they lay their eggs in the shallows. Darter larvae live in the watery silt until adulthood. Keen spotters will find darters all over the United Kingdom but most are seen in Wales, south west England and west of Scotland. You may also score points if you see one of the other darter dragonflies with blue or green body markings.

## LACEWING

**Points: 15**

**Scientific name**
*Family Chrysopidae*

Lacewings get their name from the network of veins in their wings. Although they look delicate, they have strong jaws and feed on aphids and other tiny insects.

**Points: 25**     **Top Spot!**

## ALDERFLY

**Scientific name**
*Family Megaloptera*

Alderflies are found in large numbers in early summer on waterside plants where the females lay large batches of eggs. Like those of Lacewings, their wings have a network of visible veins.

## CADDISFLY

**Points: 15**

**Scientific name**
*Philopotamus montanus*

Caddisflies look rather like moths but they have hairs on their wings instead of scales. They feed on nectar and most kinds are active at night.

**Points: 15**

## COMMON SCORPION FLY

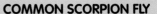

**Scientific name**
*Panorpa spp.*

These insects are quite harmless despite their name, which is derived from the appearance of the male shown here. They actually eat plant sap and dead insects.

### GREEN DRAKE MAYFLY

Top Spot!   Points: 25

**Scientific name**
*Ephemera spp.*

Most kinds of mayflies appear as adults (the winged insects) in May. They usually only live long enough to find a mate – up to about four days.

### SMALL YELLOW SALLY STONEFLY

Points: 25   Top Spot!

**Scientific name**
*Chloroperla torrentium*

Adult Stoneflies are usually found close to running water and, although they can fly, they often spend much of their time hiding among plants.

## SILVERFISH

**Points: 15**

**Scientific name**
*Lepisma saccharina*

Silverfish belong to an ancient group of insects called bristletails. Silverfish often live in nooks and crannies in kitchens where they come out at night to feed on food scraps.

**Points: 5**

## COMMON EARWIG

**Scientific name**
*Forficula auricularia*

Earwigs get their name from the mistaken idea that they will crawl into people's ears. They do usually hide in small crevices and do not often fly, even though they can!

## SPECKLED BUSH-CRICKET

Points: 15 ☆

**Scientific name**
*Leptophyes punctatissima*

Bush-Crickets look like
Grasshoppers with long
feelers but they do not
jump as freely, preferring
to walk around the plants
on which they feed.

Points: 5

## MEADOW GRASSHOPPER

**Scientific name**
*Chorthippus parallelus*

Grasshoppers are
usually found in
grassland. They 'sing'
by rubbing their legs
against a hard vein on
their front wings.

## FOREST BUG

Top Spot!          Points: 25

Scientific name *Pentatoma rufipes*

Forest Bugs are a type of Shieldbug. Shieldbugs have a distinctive shield shape and come in a variety of colours. They are also known as 'Stink Bugs' because of the very strong and unpleasant smell they produce.

Points: 15

## DOCK BUG

Scientific name *Coreus marginatus*

As its name implies this bug is commonly found on docks and sorrels, on seeds of which the young bugs feed. It may be seen across much of southern Britain and as far north as the south midlands.

## POTATO CAPSID BUG

Points: 10

Scientific name *Family Miridae*

There are many species of capsid bug, most with the general shape shown here. The Potato Capsid is often found in gardens where it likes to sit at the centre of cultivated members of the daisy family.

## ALDER SPITTLEBUG, A FROGHOPPER

**Points: 10**

**Scientific name**
*Aphrophora alni*

The froghopper is a kind of bug so-named because it tends to sit froglike with the head raised. This species is found on a wide variety of plants and can be common in gardens.

**Points: 10**
double with answer

**SPITTLEBUGS**

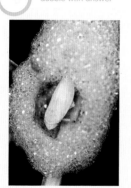

**Scientific name**
*Cercopidae*

These are young froghoppers, also called cuckoo-spit insects, because they stop themselves from drying up and hide by surrounding their bodies with a kind of froth.

*Why should the froth be called 'Cuckoo-spit'?*

14

## BLACK-AND-RED FROGHOPPER

Top Spot!  Points: 20

Scientific name
*Cercopis vulnerata*

A strikingly marked species of froghopper, the black and red colours indicating that it is probably distasteful and predators should avoid it. Numbers vary considerably from year to year.

Points: 5

## PEA APHIDS

Scientific name
*Acyrthosiphon pisum*

Aphids are tiny plant bugs, which feed on a wide variety of plants and many of them are pests. Score for any species that you come across during your searches.

## GATEKEEPER BUTTERFLY

Points: 5

**Scientific name**
*Pyronia tithonus*

The Gatekeeper Butterfly is quite common. It is also known as the Hedge Brown, which suggests where it is most often to be seen.

Points: 5

## MEADOW BROWN BUTTERFLY

**Scientific name**
*Maniola jurtina*

This is a common butterfly of rough grassland, appearing in early summer. Like all of the British brown butterflies, its caterpillars feed on the long grasses of meadows and overgrown gardens.

## RINGLET BUTTERFLY

**Points: 15**

**Scientific name**
*Aphantopus hyperantus*

The Ringlet is a dark brown butterfly and it gets its name from the black and white circles on the undersides of its wings.

**Points: 10**

## SPECKLED WOOD BUTTERFLY

**Scientific name**
*Pararge aegeria*

The brown and yellow markings on the wings of this butterfly make it hard to see as it flits among the trees.

## SMALL PEARL-BORDERED FRITILLARY BUTTERFLY

**Top Spot!** **Points: 20** for any fritillary

**Scientific name**

*Boloria selene*

These butterflies get their name because of the pattern of spots on an orangey background. They tend to live in small colonies by

woods or in open country. Small Pearl-bordered Frittilarys have been in decline throughout Britain over the last few years, but you can still spot them in western Scotland, southern England and parts of Wales.

Points: 5

## SMALL TORTOISESHELL BUTTERFLY

**Scientific name** *Aglais urticae*

Found in abundance across most of Britain, the Small Tortoiseshell appears in early summer and is often seen on the 'Butterfly Bush', the buddleia. Its caterpillars feed on nettles.

## MARBLED WHITE BUTTERFLY

Points: 15

**Scientific name** *Melanargia galathea*

Despite its name, the Marbled White is in the same family as the brown butterflies and is not related to the Cabbage Whites. It is found in rough pasture during mid-summer.

Points: 10

## RED ADMIRAL BUTTERFLY

**Scientific name** *Vanessa atalanta*

This large, brightly coloured butterfly is usually first seen in May or June but, although it is a Mediterranean insect, some individuals do manage to survive the harsh British winter.

### PAINTED LADY BUTTERFLY

**Points: 15**

**Scientific name**
*Vanessa cardui*

A migrant from the Mediterranean, the Painted Lady usually appears in Britain around May or June. This brightly coloured butterfly lays its eggs on thistles and nettles.

**Points: 15**

### COMMA BUTTERFLY

**Scientific name**
*Polygonia c-album*

Pale comma-shaped markings on the underwings give this butterfly its name. Usually found in woodlands, its distinctive tattered-looking wings act as camouflage against predators.

## PEACOCK BUTTERFLY

**Points: 10**
double with answer

**Scientific name**
*Aglais io*

This large, brightly coloured insect may be seen during April and May and then again in September and October.

*How does it get its name?*

**Points: 15**

## LARGE SKIPPER BUTTERFLY

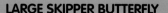

**Scientific name**
*Ochlodes sylvanus*

Skippers look more like moths than butterflies. They get their name because they beat their wings quickly and 'skip' from place to place so they are hard to spot.

## COMMON BLUE BUTTERFLY

**Points: 15**

**Scientific name**
*Polyommatus icarus*

Common Blue butterflies are found on open grassland, commons, heaths and downs across most of mainland Britain. The female Common Blue is a brownish colour.

**Points: 10**

## ORANGE-TIP BUTTERFLY

**Scientific name**
*Anthocharis cardamines*

The Orange-tip is a member of the white butterfly family. The male exhibits the distinctive orange-tipped forewings that give the species its name, however the female is almost entirely white.

Points: 25    Top Spot!

## CLOUDED YELLOW BUTTERFLY

**Scientific name**
*Colias croceus*

Usually a rare sight even in southern Britain, the Clouded Yellow is another migrant from continental Europe or north Africa. Lava and pupa are susceptible to frost and so new generations rarely survive British winters.

## LARGE WHITE BUTTERFLY

**Points: 5**
for any white species

**Scientific name**
*Pieris brassicae*

The Large White is the largest of the three common species of white butterflies found in the British Isles. The other two are the Small White and the Green-Veined White, the latter of which has noticeable lines on the underwings.

## BUTTERFLY CHRYSALIS

Top Spot! Points: 25

25

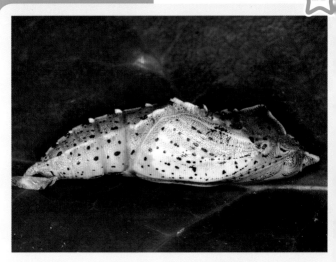

The life cycles of most butterflies and moths have distinct stages. Butterflies lay eggs, from which larvae in the form of caterpillars emerge. When the time is right, usually after months of feeding and growing these caterpillars attach themselves to leaves or branches for the next stage of the process. They gradually shed their outer skins to reveal a hard shell called a chrysalis underneath. Inside the chrysalis the caterpillar transforms into a butterfly in a process known as metamorphosis. It can take many days or even weeks before the adult butterfly emerges. Chrysalises vary in size, shape and colour from species to species. This chrysalis is of a Large White Butterfly.

**Points: 15**

## PEPPERED MOTH CATERPILLAR

**Scientific name**
*Biston betularia*

The long, stick-like caterpillars of the Peppered Moth have three pairs of legs at the front of the body and four 'claspers' at the back with no legs between. They move by 'looping', a kind of crawling motion which involves the caterpillar creating a loop in its body to drag itself forward.

## SIX-SPOT BURNET MOTH

**Points: 10**

**Scientific name**
*Zygaena filipendulae*

The burnets are day-fliers when they can often be found visiting flowers to feed. Their bright colours warn possible predators that they are not good to eat. The caterpillars take in the poison from the plants on which they feed.

25

## PRIVET HAWK MOTH

Top Spot!    Points: 20

**Scientific name**
*Sphinx ligustri*

Wherever privet hedges grow so you are likely to find this large moth. When disturbed it opens its wings to reveal pink markings as a warning to predators.

**Points: 15**
for either elephant hawk moth

## LARGE ELEPHANT HAWK MOTH

**Scientific name**
*Deilephila elpenor*

This very beautiful moth is fairly common and can usually be found in gardens from May onwards. The Small Elephant Hawk Moth is similar but with less pink on the wings.

## LARGE ELEPHANT HAWK MOTH CATERPILLAR

**Points: 10**

**Scientific name**
*Deilephila elpenor*

This very striking caterpillar, which may be mistaken for a small snake, reaches 90 mm (3½ in) in length and feeds on willowherb.

**Points: 25**   **Top Spot!**

## HUMMINGBIRD HAWK MOTH

**Scientific name**
*Macroglossum stellatarum*

The adult moth hovers in front of a flower and uses its long coiled tongue to collect nectar. Some people actually think they have seen a humming bird when they spot this visitor from Europe.

## EYED HAWK MOTH

Top Spot! Points: 20

**Scientific name**
*Smerinthus ocellatus*

When at rest, this moth sits with its wings closed but when disturbed it opens its forewings to reveal hindwings with eye-marks on them as a way of surprising a predator.

 Points: 15

## EYED HAWK MOTH CATERPILLAR

**Scientific name**
*Smerinthus ocellatus*

The main food plants of this caterpillar are willows, sallows and apple, so look for it on the apple trees in your garden or orchard. Like many hawk moth caterpillars, it has a horn on the tail.

**Points: 25**    Top Spot!

## BUFF-TIP MOTH

**Scientific name**
*Phalera bucephala*

Buff-tip Moths look a bit like a broken stick when they are at rest. They are sometimes called smudge moths because of their dull colouring.

## BUFF-TIP MOTH CATERPILLAR

**Points: 10**

**Scientific name**
*Phalera bucephala*

These hairy caterpillars stay together in a group when small, splitting up as they get bigger. Look for them on oak, elm, lime and hazel trees.

## GARDEN TIGER MOTH

Top Spot! Points: 25

**Scientific name**
*Arctia caja*

Tiger moths taste unpleasant and the bright colours of the moth's hindwings warn birds to leave them alone. The pattern of the forewings probably helps to break up the insect's outline.

**Points: 10**

### GARDEN TIGER MOTH CATERPILLAR

**Scientific name** *Arctia caja*

You are actually much more likely to come across a 'woolly bear', (the nickname for a tiger moth caterpillar), than find the adult moth. They feed on a wide variety of plants and are often found in gardens.

### CINNABAR MOTH

**Points: 15**

**Scientific name** *Tyria jacobaea*

The brightly coloured Cinnabar Moth is again warning birds that it is poisonous and they should not try to eat it. These moths fly by day and night.

**Points: 5**

### CINNABAR MOTH CATERPILLAR

**Scientific name** *Tyria jacobaea*

There is no mistaking the black-and-yellow striped caterpillars of the Cinnabar Moth. One of their favourite foods is ragwort and they are quite useful to us by destroying this plant, which is so dangerous to horses.

## BURNISHED BRASS MOTH

Top Spot! Points: 25

**Scientific name**
*Diachrysia chrysitis*

These moths are part of a very large family, which all tend to have rather dull coloured front wings. With its shiny, metallic patches this is one of the exceptions.

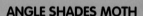

Points: 20   Top Spot!

## ANGLE SHADES MOTH

**Scientific name**
*Phlogophora meticulosa*

When at rest on a dead, brown leaf, the dull colours and patterning on the forewings of this moth make it very hard for an enemy to see.

**Points: 5**
double with answer

## MARSH BROWN-EDGED TIPULA CRANE FLY

**Scientific name**
*Tipula spp.*

Crane flies are sometimes called 'daddy-long-legs' and the weak-flying adults usually appear from summer to autumn.

*What name is given to the larva of the crane fly?*

## HOUSE GNAT

**Points: 15**

**Scientific name**
*Family Culicidae*

Small mosquitoes are often called gnats. It is the female which feeds on blood, usually that of birds. The males have hairy feelers, which they use to 'hear' the wingbeats of the females.

33

## NOTCH-HORNED CLEG

Points: 15

**Scientific name**
*Haematopota pluvialis*

Female horse flies, or clegs, drink blood by biting animals including domestic cattle. Unfortunately they will also bite humans. A horse fly bite can be painful and will cause the area to swell. Not pleasant!

 Points: 10

## BLACK-RIMMED SNOUT HOVERFLY

**Scientific name**
*Rhingia campestris*

Identifiable by its bulbous 'nose' and the black lines on its abdomen, this hoverfly is a common sight in spring and early summer. It feeds on a wide range of flowers but is especially fond of apple blossom.

## LONG HOVERFLY

**Points: 10**

**Scientific name**
*Sphaerophoria spp.*

These wasp-like insects get their name for their ability to hover in the air. They cannot sting, but their appearance fools their enemies into thinking that they are dangerous.

**Points: 15**

## SHINING-FACED DRONE FLY

**Scientific name**
*Eristalis spp.*

The drone fly is quite a good mimic of the hive bee. Like the hive bee it feeds on pollen and the two may often be found together on the same flower.

## BUMBLE BEE PLUME-HORN, A HOVERFLY

Points: 20

**Scientific name**
*Volucella bombylans*

This hoverfly has forms mimicking both white-tailed and red-tailed bumble bees. It lays its eggs in bumble bee nests, where the larvae feed on bits and pieces discarded by the bees.

**Points: 5**

**Scientific name**
*Calliphora spp.*

Male Bluebottles feed on nectar but the female often buzzes loudly into the house in search of meat on which to lay its eggs. These flies may spend the winter hiding in houses.

**GREENBOTTLE FLY**

**Points: 5**

**Scientific name**
*Lucilia caesar*

Like Bluebottles, Greenbottles are 'blow flies', for when they lay their eggs on meat, the maggots feed on the meat – it is then said to be 'blown'.

# FLIES

## COMMON HOUSE FLY

**Points: 5**

**Scientific name** *Musca domestica*

This fly is always an unwanted visitor to our homes, since it can spread germs of one kind or another. It can be easily confused with the lesser house fly which is smaller and is the one which flies in circles around ceiling lights.

**Points: 10**

## COMMON YELLOW DUNG FLY

**Scientific name** *Scathophaga stercoraria*

As its name suggests, the female of this bright-yellow furry-looking fly lays its eggs on cattle droppings. When they hatch, the grubs feed on the dung, helping to break down the manure.

## COMMON AWL ROBBER FLY

**Points: 15**

**Scientific name** *Family Asilidae*

Robber flies feed by attacking other insects and sucking out the contents of their bodies. They have stiff hairs on their legs, which help them to grip on to their victims.

Points: 25  Top Spot!

**Scientific name**
*Rhagio tringarius*

It is generally thought that these rather 'wasp-like' flies prey on other insects. Snipe fly larvae live on the ground and eat beetles and worms.

## DARK-EDGED BEE-FLY

**Top Spot! Points: 20** ⭐

**Scientific name**
*Bombylius major*

Look out for this fly from early spring onwards, when it may be found visiting flowers such as celandine and primrose. Note how it hovers in mid-air as it feeds on nectar with its long proboscis.

**Points: 15**

## FLESH FLY

**Scientific name**
*Scathophaga spp.*

The common Flesh Fly gets its name from the fact that its larvae sometimes feed on the flesh of open wounds. The adult flies are attracted to the smell of rotting meat and faeces.

Points: 10

## ST MARK'S FLY

**Scientific name**
*Bibio marci*

During spring and early summer these flies can be very numerous. They are very clumsy in flight and the males have much bigger eyes than the females.

## NOONDAY FLY

Points: 15

**Scientific name**
*Mesembrina meridiana*

Look for the adult fly on flowers, especially brambles, in late summer and autumn. You may also find them on cow dung, where they lay their eggs. Their maggots eat the larvae of other insects feeding on the dung.

41

## DANCE FLY

Points: 15

**Scientific name**
*Empis livida*

Dance Fly adults feed mainly on other flies, which they catch in mid-air and spear on their long proboscis. The larvae which are found in moist soil and rotten wood, are also carnivorous.

Points: 10

## SMALL FRUIT FLY

**Scientific name**
*Family Drosophilidae*

These little flies are especially attracted to rotting fruit and vegetables and can turn up in huge numbers on compost heaps. They may also be seen buzzing around the top of an open wine bottle.

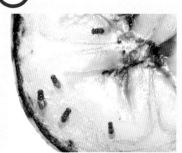

### BLACK ANT

**Points: 5**
double score for winged males
and females leaving the nest

**Scientific name**
*Lasius spp.*

Look for the Black Ant in your garden and do not forget that it is the female worker ants which have no wings; the Queen ant and the males have wings and can fly.

**Points: 10**

### YELLOW MEADOW ANTS

**Scientific name**
*Lasius flavus*

Meadow ants nest in a mound. They keep root aphids in their nest, which are kept in 'herds' like cows so that the ants can feed on the honeydew, which the aphids produce.

## ANT'S NEST

Top Spot!    Points: 25

Some ants are nomadic and do not build permanent homes, but many build complex nests to live in. Some are underground but others can be seen on top of the ground or even in trees.

**Points: 15**

### WOOD ANT

**Scientific name** *Formica rufa*

The huge mound of leaves, sticks and other plant material is the nest of the Wood Ant. It favours dry woodland for its nest and is our biggest ant.

### GERMAN WASP

**Points: 5**

**Scientific name** *Vespula germanica*

Wasps build nests made from a papery material made by chewing up pieces of wood. German Wasps differ from Common Wasps by having three dots on their face as well as more clearly defined dots on their abdomens.

**Points: 15**

### RUBY-TAILED WASP

**Scientific name** *Family Chrysididae*

These little insects are not that uncommon and will be found on walls and fences searching for the nest holes of solitary wasps or other species in which to lay their eggs.

### HORNET

**Top Spot!**    **Points: 20**

**Scientific name**
*Vespa crabro vexator*

Although these brown and orange wasps are bigger than the more common black and yellow wasps, they are not usually aggressive and will rarely sting people.

**Points: 10**

### BUFF-TAILED BUMBLE BEE

**Scientific name**
*Bombus terrestris*

Bumble bees live in smaller colonies than honeybees. Some workers suck up nectar while others collect pollen. As they pass from flower to flower, they pollinate the plants. Only the queen has the distinctive buff coloured abdomen tip; on the workers they are white.

**Points: 5**
double with answer

## HONEYBEE

**Scientific name**
*Apis mellifera*

There may be many thousands of worker bees (females that cannot breed) in one hive. The workers defend the nest and collect nectar, which they feed to the bee grubs.

*What are male bees called?*

## LARGE GARDEN LEAFCUTTER BEE

**Points: 15**

**Scientific name**
*Megachile spp.*

Round or oval lumps cut out of the leaves of roses and other garden plants are usually the work of leafcutter bees. The bits of leaf are used to make chambers, which they fill with pollen to feed their developing larvae.

Points: 15

## SANGUINE MINING BEE

**Scientific name** *Andrena haemorrhoa*

Look out for tiny volcanoes on lawns and at the side of earth paths, for these are the nest entrances of mining bees. If you are lucky you will see the female peering out from the entrance, as here.

## WOOL CARDER BEE

Points: 15

**Scientific name** *Anthidium manicatum*

The appearance of the Wool Carder Bee tends to coincide with the flowering of the woundworts in our gardens and hedgerows. Watch out for the larger male as he patrols a patch of these plants, often hovering in mid air.

Points: 10

## RED MASON BEE

**Scientific name** *Osmia bicornis*

This springtime bee is so-called because it often builds its mud nest in cracks in old masonry. It is more common to see the female Mason Bee as the male dies soon after mating.

**Points: 15**

## DEVIL'S COACH HORSE BEETLE

**Scientific name**
*Ocypus olens*

You are more likely to see this beetle at night unless you disturb one from under a stone. But beware, the Devil's Coach Horse is aggressive and can inflict a painful bite.

**Points: 15**
double with answer

## COCKCHAFER

**Scientific name**
*Melolontha melolontha*

A large beetle that emerges in May or June. You can spot them by the distinctive 'leaves' at the end of their antennae.

*What other common name is given to them?*

49

## SOLDIER BEETLE

**Points: 10**

**Scientific name**
*Rhagonycha fulva*

These colourful beetles are fairly easy to spot. They are active in the daytime and found across the whole country. Their nickname is 'bloodsucker', even though they are harmless to humans.

**Points: 15**

## BUMBLE-DOR BEETLE

**Scientific name**
*Family Geotrupidae*

Dor beetle larvae feed on dung. The word 'dor' comes from an Old English word which means 'buzzing insect' or even 'bumble bee' and, when they are in flight, dor beetles do make a buzzing noise.

## SEVEN-SPOT LADYBIRD

Points: 5

**Scientific name**
*Coccinella
septempunctata*

Everyone knows the
ladybird. There are
both red and yellow
species with different
numbers of spots. The
bright colours warn
enemies that they are
unpleasant to eat.

Points: 15

## RED-HEADED CARDINAL BEETLE

**Scientific name**
*Pyrochroa serraticornis*

There are three species of
cardinal beetle in Britain.
This one has a red head
whereas the other two
types have black heads.
All of them live on the
edges of woodlands and
eat small insects.

### SPOTTED LONGHORN BEETLE

**Points: 15**
double with answer

**Scientific name** *Rutpela maculata*

This very common beetle is a ready flier and is best sought for around flowering brambles, where it feeds from the flowers.

*Why is it called a longhorn beetle?*

**Points: 15**

### CLICK BEETLE

**Scientific name** *Family Elateridae*

Called a Click Beetle because of the click which can be heard when escaping from predators. Pick one up and not only will you hear the click but you will also see how effective the system is.

### WASP BEETLE

**Points: 10**

**Scientific name** *Clytus arietis*

The Wasp Beetle is well-named for it does indeed resemble a wasp at first glance. It is usually found around trees and if you are lucky you may find a female laying her eggs into old wood.

Points: 20    Top Spot!

**BURYING BEETLE**

**Scientific name**
*Nicrophorus spp.*

Also called a sexton beetle this insect is associated with the corpses of dead animals upon which it lays its eggs and on which its larvae feed. Not nice to look for but interesting all the same.

## GREEN TORTOISE BEETLE

**Points: 15**
for any tortoise beetle

**Scientific name**
*Cassida viridis*

Look for this beetle on white dead-nettle and mints. A very similar looking species can be found on creeping thistles. Both are well camouflaged and not easy to find.

**Points: 10**

## THICK-LEGGED FLOWER BEETLE MALE

**Scientific name**
*Oedemera nobilis*

This beetle can be very common in early summer and is best looked for on yellow flowers such as dandelions and its relations. The female is a dull green and does not have thick legs.

## Points: 10

### VIOLET GROUND BEETLE

**Scientific name** *Carabus spp.*

The Violet Ground Beetle is the gardener's and farmer's friend for it feeds on slugs. It gets its name because it has a purple appearance when seen from certain angles.

### BLACK OIL BEETLE

## Points: 15

**Scientific name** *Meloe spp.*

Also called blister beetles, it is best not to handle them for they release an unpleasant liquid used to warn off anything which tries to eat them.

## Points: 10
for any long snouted weevil

### ACORN WEEVIL

**Scientific name** *Curculio venosus*

Weevils are beetles that have their biting jaws on the end of a snout, which can vary in length depending on the species. The Acorn Weevil is one of the long snouted types.

### WOODLICE

**Points: 5**
double with answer

**Scientific name**
*Oniscus asellus*

Woodlice are not insects; they are related to crabs and lobsters. During the day they hide in cool, dark places and come out at night to feed.

*How many legs does a Woodlouse have?*

**Points: 15**

### SEA SLATER

**Scientific name**
*Ligia oceanica*

You will have to be beside the sea to find this relative of the Woodlouse. It lives on rocks and cliffs above the high tide line.

## WIRE-LEGGED HARVESTMAN

**Points: 10**

**Scientific name**
*Order Opiliones*

Although they resemble spiders and are related to them, harvestmen are not 'true spiders'. One way to tell the difference is to count the eyes. Harvestmen only have two eyes but most spiders have more.

 **Points: 5**

## GIANT HOUSE SPIDER

**Scientific name**
*Erategina/Tegenaria spp.*

Despite its name, the Giant House Spider can be found in the garden under rocks and logs as often as in the house. Females are larger than males and may reach almost 2 cm (3/4 in) in body length.

## CELLAR SPIDER

**Points: 10**

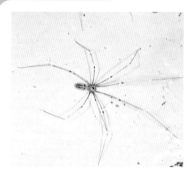

Scientific name
*Pholcus phalangioides*

This easily recognisable spider builds its untidy web in the corner of houses, sheds and garages where the temperature is not likely to drop below 10°C (50°F). It often feeds on the much larger house spider.

**Points: 15**

## GARDEN SPIDER

Scientific name
*Araneus diadematus*

This spider may vary in colour from pale brown to reddish-ginger. It is found in gardens, woodlands, and heathlands. Look out for the white markings on its back, which form a cross shape.

## COMMON FLOWER SPIDER

Points: 20    Top Spot!

Scientific name *Misumena vatia*

This crab spider is usually found on flowers, where it lies in wait to catch its prey. It has the ability to change colour to yellow and back to white, the change taking a few hours to complete.

## SPOTTED WOLF SPIDER

Points: 5

Scientific name *Pardosa spp.*

These spiders get their name because it was once thought that they hunted in packs. They do run along the ground very quickly but are most often found 'sunbathing' on a suitable log or stone.

Points: 10

## SPIDER'S WEB

Many spiders spin webs to catch prey. Search for webs on dewy mornings when they can look quite spectacular.

## STONE CENTIPEDE

**Points: 10**

**Scientific name**
*Lithobius spp.*

You can sometimes find centipedes hiding under stones or logs. Despite their name, which means '100 legs', they can have as few as 34 legs or as many as 300 or more!

**Points: 15**

## STRIPED MILLIPEDE

**Scientific name**
*Ommatoiulus sabulosus*

There are many varieties of millipede found hiding under logs and under rocks across the UK. This one has two long stripes down its length. Millipedes differ from centipedes by having two sets of legs on each body segment instead of one.

## TOOTHED PONDSKATER BUG

**Points: 15**

**Scientific name**
*Gerris odontogaster*

Pondskaters are also known as the waterstriders. The middle pair of legs is much longer than the others and is used to 'row' the insect across the surface of the water.

**Points: 25**    **Top Spot!**

## WATER MEASURER

**Scientific name**
*Hydrometra stagnorum*

This insect gets its name from the way it carefully walks along the surface of the water at the edge of a pond. It feeds on water fleas, mosquito larvae and small, drowned insects.

## WHIRLIGIG BEETLE

**Points: 15**

**Scientific name**
*Gyrinus substriatus*

Whirligig Beetles are found on the open areas of ponds, where groups of them scoot around the surface in an almost endless movement searching for small prey below and on the surface of the water.

**Points: 10**

## AMBER SNAIL

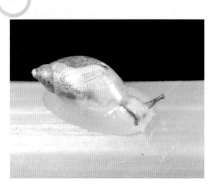

**Scientific name**
*Succinea putris*

Look for this snail with its rather glass-like shell on plants beside ponds, streams, rivers and canals. They can be found all over the UK but are more common in the south.

Answers: P3 Earthworms feed on rotting vegetable matter. P14 They first appear around the time that the cuckoo returns to Britain. P21 The eyespots on the wings are similar to those on the tail feathers of the bird of the same name. P33 The larva is called a leatherjacket. P47 Male bees are called drones. P49 They are called may bugs. P52 Because it has very long antennae, its 'feelers'. P56 They have five pairs of legs.

# i-SPY

## How to get your i-SPY certificate and badge

Let us know when you've become a Super-Spotter with 1000 points and we'll send you a special certificate and badge!

## HERE'S WHAT TO DO!

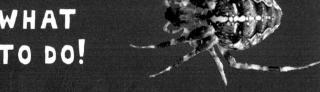

- Ask an adult to check your score.

- Visit www.collins.co.uk/i-SPY to apply for your certificate. If you are under the age of 13 you will need a parent or guardian to do this.

- We'll send your certificate via email and you'll receive a brilliant badge through the post!